The Addiction to People: The Quiet Rebellion of Solitude

ISBN: 978-1-9194919-5-0 - paperback

ISBN: 978-1-9194919-4-3 - eBook

ISBN: 978-1-9194919-6-7 - hardcover

The Addiction To People

The Quiet Rebellion of Solitude

Sand Books
Book 1

Caterina Mondragon

Foreword

This book is gently shaped to shift how you see.

Take it slowly.

A single line is enough.

Let it sit with you.

Let it unfold in its own time.

There is nothing to complete here, only something to notice within yourself.

Read when you can.

Reflect, internalise, and, if it feels right, practice.

If something changes, even quietly, that is enough.

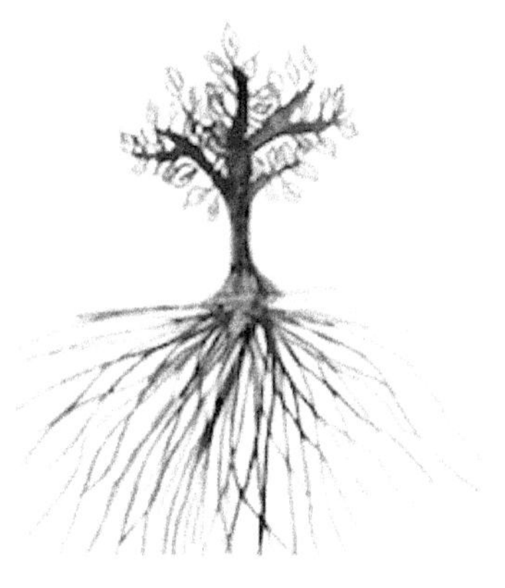

"The greatest thing in the world is to know how to belong to oneself."

Michel de Montaigne

Introduction

We are not afraid of being alone.

We are afraid of what it might reveal.

This book is a quiet exploration of that fear and of the freedom that begins when it is no longer there.

I

The Fear of Being Alone

"All of humanity's problems stem from man's inability to sit quietly in a room alone."

Blaise Pascal

"Loneliness expresses the pain of being alone and solitude expresses the glory of being alone."

Paul Tillich

"The worst loneliness is not to be comfortable with yourself."

Mark Twain

"We live as we dream — alone."

Joseph Conrad

"The eternal quest of the individual human being is to shatter his loneliness."

Norman Cousins

"What loneliness is more lonely than distrust?"

George Eliot

“People are lonely because they build walls instead of bridges.”

Joseph F. Newton

"The strongest man in the world is he who stands most alone."

Henrik Ibsen

"Language has created the word loneliness to
express the pain of being alone."

Paul Tillich

II
The Myth of Belonging

"Friendship is a single soul dwelling in two bodies."

Aristotle

"The meeting of two personalities is like the contact of two chemical substances."

Carl Jung

"The beginning of love is to let those we love be perfectly themselves."

Thomas Merton

"We accept the love we think we deserve."

Stephen Chbosky

“A true friend is someone who lets you have total freedom to be yourself.”

Jim Morrison

“Attachment is the great fabricator of illusions.”

Simone Weil

"Love does not consist in gazing at each other, but in looking outward together."

Antoine de Saint-Exupéry

III

Together Yet Lonely

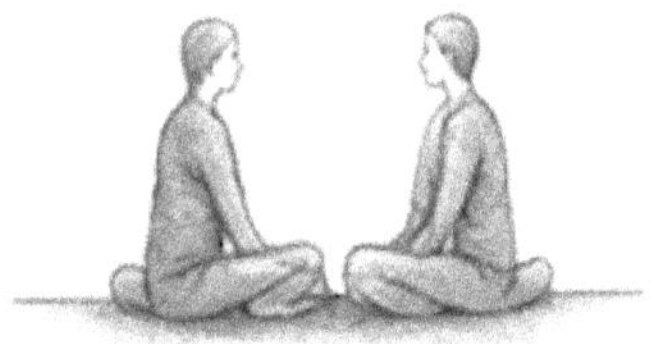

"Loneliness does not come from having no people around you."

Carl Jung

"We are for the most part more lonely when we go abroad among men."

Henry David Thoreau

"All great and precious things are lonely."

John Steinbeck

"Solitude is not measured by the miles of space between a man and his fellows."

Henry David Thoreau

"What a lovely surprise to discover how unlovely being alone can be."

Ellen Burstyn

"I restore myself when I'm alone."

Marilyn Monroe

"I never found the companion that was so companionable as solitude."

Henry David Thoreau

"One can be instructed in society, one is inspired only in solitude."

Goethe

VI

The Fear of Silence

"Who looks outside dreams; who looks inside awakes."

Carl Jung

"The quieter you become, the more you can hear."

Ram Dass

"Silence is a source of great strength."

Lao Tzu

"Your vision will become clear only when you look into your own heart."

Carl Jung

"No one saves us but ourselves."

Buddha

"The unexamined life is not worth living."

Socrates

"Knowing yourself is the beginning of wisdom."

Aristotle

“Peace comes from within.”

Buddha

"Until you make the unconscious conscious, it will direct your life."

Carl Jung

V

The Comparison Trap

"Comparison is the thief of joy."

Theodore Roosevelt

"Whenever you find yourself on the side of the majority, pause."

Mark Twain

"The crowd is untruth."

Søren Kierkegaard

"The mass of men lead lives of quiet desperation."

Henry David Thoreau

"Care about what other people think and you will always be their prisoner."

Lao Tzu

“No one can make you feel inferior without your consent.”

Eleanor Roosevelt

"Public opinion is a weak tyrant."

Harriet Martineau

"To avoid criticism, say nothing, do nothing, be nothing."

Elbert Hubbard

"The individual is the smallest minority on earth."

Ayn Rand

VI
Learning to Sit with Yourself

"Solitude is independence."

Hermann Hesse

"In solitude the mind gains strength."

Laurence Sterne

"All of humanity's problems stem from man's inability to sit quietly in a room alone."

Blaise Pascal

"The more powerful and original a mind, the more it will incline toward solitude."

Arthur Schopenhauer

“The best thinking has been done in solitude.”

Thomas Edison

"Originality thrives in seclusion free of outside influences."

Nikola Tesla

"All truly great thoughts are conceived while walking."

Friedrich Nietzsche

"The monotony and solitude of a quiet life stimulates the creative mind."

Albert Einstein

"A man can be himself only so long as he is alone."

Arthur Schopenhauer

VII
Independence

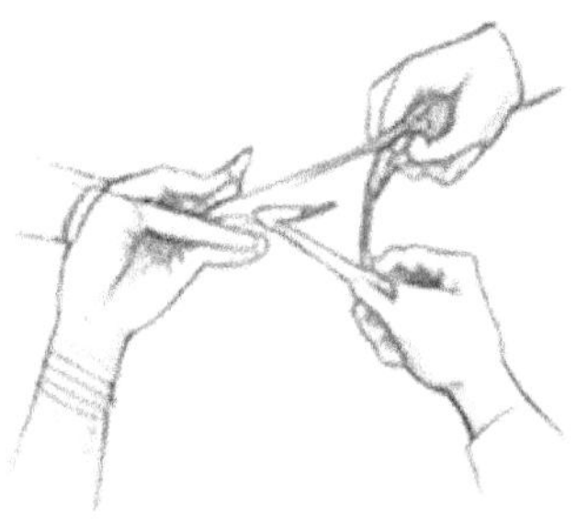

"No man is free who is not master of himself."

Epictetus

"He who conquers himself is the mightiest warrior."

Confucius

"You have power over your mind, not outside events."

Marcus Aurelius

"The only way to deal with an unfree world is to become so absolutely free..."

Albert Camus

"Man is disturbed not by things, but by the views he takes of them."

Epictetus

"Knowing others is intelligence; knowing yourself is true wisdom."

Lao Tzu

“Freedom lies in being bold.”

Robert Frost

"The happiness of your life depends upon the quality of your thoughts."

Marcus Aurelius

VIII
Choosing Relationships Freely

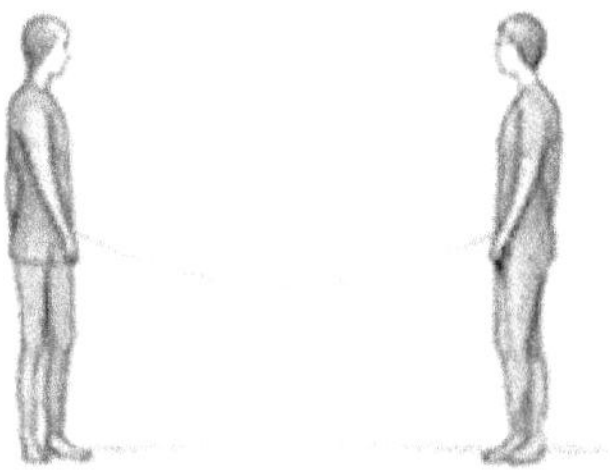

"Love consists in this, that two solitudes protect and touch each other."

Rainer Maria Rilke

"To love at all is to be vulnerable."

C. S. Lewis

"Love is the only sane and satisfactory answer to human existence."

Erich Fromm

"Love is not about possession. Love is about appreciation."

Osho

"Friendship is always a sweet responsibility."

Khalil Gibran

"A healthy relationship keeps the doors and windows open."

Bob Dylan

"The opposite of loneliness is not company; it is intimacy."

Richard Bach

IX

The Quiet Power of Solitude

"The soul that sees beauty may sometimes walk alone."

Goethe

"To live alone is the fate of all great souls."

Schopenhauer

“Solitude is the nurse of wisdom.”

Laurence Sterne

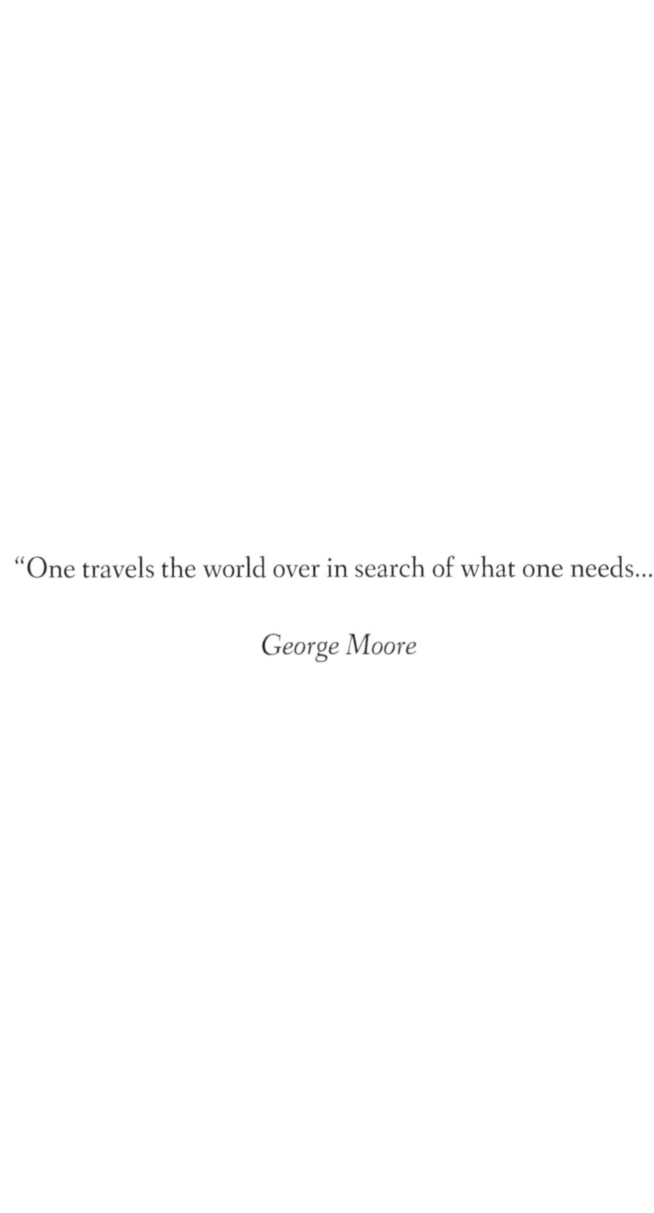

"One travels the world over in search of what one needs..."

George Moore

“The journey inward is the longest journey.”

Dag Hammarskjöld

“The quieter you become, the more you are able to hear.”

Ram Dass

"Silence is sometimes the best answer."

Dalai Lama

When you are no longer afraid of being alone, you are finally free to choose who truly belongs in your life.

Epilogue

When you are no longer afraid of being alone, you are free to choose who truly belongs in your life.

Nothing is missing. Nothing was ever missing. You were never incomplete, only afraid.

You do not need to be chosen. You only need to choose.

Choose yourself.

Always.

www.ingramcontent.com/pod-product-compliance
Lightning Source LLC
LaVergne TN
LVHW010105110826
845155LV00028B/485